DYNAMISM OR DECAY?

Dynamism or Decay? Getting City Hall Out of the Way
Volume Two

Sal Rodriguez

January 2023

ISBN: 978-1-934276-50-1

Pacific Research Institute
P.O. Box 60485
Pasadena, CA 91116

www.pacificresearch.org

Nothing contained in this report is to be construed as necessarily reflecting the views of the Pacific Research Institute or as an attempt to thwart or aid the passage of any legislation. The views expressed remain solely the authors'. They are not endorsed by any of the authors' past or present affiliations.

DYNAMISM OR DECAY?
GETTING CITY HALL
OUT OF THE WAY

By Sal Rodriguez

VOLUME TWO

PR PACIFIC
RESEARCH
INSTITUTE

Cities are complex, emergent systems that attract and enable anywhere from thousands to millions of people to live and work among each other mostly peacefully and mostly productively. They are capable of accommodating people with incredibly diverse needs, interests, wishes, occupations, consumer preferences and lifestyles.

Think of any reasonably sized city.

Diverse bars, cafes and restaurants pop up to serve the gastronomic interests of residents and visitors. Bike shops and car dealerships serve transportation needs. Big and small retailers provide a litany of consumer goods. Grocery chains, mom-and-pop shops, convenience and liquor stores provide a litany of items.

A range of housing types with distinct styles, functions and arrangements will exist to serve the needs, budgets and preferences of people living very different lives. Multiple options for internet service and mobile phone providers to connect you to the world.

Beyond sources of places to buy goods and services, there will be religious centers of various kinds – churches, mosques, synagogues – as well as nonprofit organizations and volunteer groups formed to address issues in a given community.

No amount of centralized planning and coordination could pull off all of the things that make great cities great. No one can know all of the interests or needs of hundreds of thousands or millions of people, nor could any one person know how best to deliver what people want.

Critical in this complicated dynamic is the role of city governments. One responsibility of municipal governments is to establish and enforce rules and regulations. Another is to either directly provide or arrange the provision of certain services.

How city governments handle these fundamental tasks can either facilitate or stifle the dynamism of their respective jurisdictions.

Simple, easy-to-follow rules allow people to pursue their own interests within clear and certain frameworks. Convoluted, restrictive rules can deter, slow or stop people from pursuing their own interests.

How city governments handle their rule-setting responsibility can make the difference between whether people can set up businesses in the first place or decide to expand within city limits. City ordinances and permitting processes can determine whether or not homes get built, what types of homes get built and how affordable they really are. Likewise, when public services are provided with customer service, effectiveness and fiscal responsibility in mind, city residents will generally not only appreciate the service but also get their money's worth.

By contrast, when the guiding light of the provision of public services is no longer the best interests of the public that's being served, city residents can find themselves subject to a poorer level of service, even at a higher price. Unlike with the litany of services sought and received from the private sector, what city hall delivers is all you're going to get. There are no other choices.

Arbitrary or preferential exercises of these respective powers can distort and skew matters further – and there are myriad ways this can happen. Cities are subject to the advantages and risks that come with any domain of life that is subject to the political process.

The typical city is overseen by politicians with their own incentives, which can easily be distorted by the political process. In economics, "public choice theory" postulates that government officials don't act out of some inchoate "public good" – but are individuals who maximize their own self-interest. And that interest doesn't often yield the best results for captive city residents.

From big businesses looking for an edge over competitors to unions looking to capitalize on government monopolies, it usually doesn't take much for a city to head in the wrong direction.

Meanwhile, politicians elected to oversee cities in turn delegate responsibilities to bureaucrats, who have their own incentives to engage in featherbedding and mission creep. The longer this goes on, the more entrenched it becomes, the more city governments resemble not earnest service-providers to those who chose to live their lives in city limits but politically captured entities which do the bidding of whoever can best influence them.

The further cities go down these roads of manipulation and control, the greater distortions to the dynamics of cities, the greater potential for misallocation of resources and the greater potential for making poor decisions, to the detriment of people just trying to live their lives and earn a living.

Over the course of this short book, I will make the case that what cities ought to do is establish basic, coherent rules, focus on their competencies, contract out services that can be done as well or better for lower costs than they can, and leave the rest to free people to sort out for themselves.

Sounds simple, right? I agree. If cities stuck to these simple and even self-evident suggestions, I wouldn't have needed to write any of these words. But city halls can be impressive in just how much they manage to get wrong.

Getting in the way of business

To start with the classic way local governments get in the way of private sector initiative, consider the arbitrariness and vast disparities in how local governments handle and process business permits. What city you're in can dictate how challenging and costly it can be to get government approval to do business.

The Institute for Justice, a nonprofit libertarian public interest law firm and advocacy organization, recently studied the process for starting up a business in 20 cities across the country, releasing their findings in a report titled, "Barriers to Business: How cities can pave a cheaper, faster and simpler path to entrepreneurship."[1]

"Starting a business is already a tough proposition," the report notes, "Entrepreneurs take considerable risks and often invest large sums of their own money – but this death by a thousand cuts from city and state rules imposes scores of additional burdens that bog down entrepreneurs with high fees, long wait times, and complex paperwork."[2]

There's often little consistency to how these processes work or how much they cost.

If you want to open a barbershop in Boise, Idaho, for example, you'll have to pay an average cost of $1,609 in licensing and permitting fees, fill out 11 forms and deal with an average of eight agencies. If you want to do the same in San Francisco, you'll have to pay an average of $14,305 in licensing and permitting fees, fill out nine forms and deal with nine agencies. In Boise, you'll have to make four in-person appearances to jump through these hoops, while San Francisco requires five.

There's nothing magical or set in stone about these fees and processes. Technology could and should be utilized to make it cheaper and easier to fill out the required paperwork. But governments have little incentive to innovate or reconsider the reasonableness of these processes without a deliberate push for them to do so.

Some cities will be reasonable in how they handle some aspects of business regulation. Seattle, for example, assesses business licenses based on their respective revenues, which helps accommodate small businesses. On the other hand, Seattle also imposes tight restrictions on small home-based businesses, physically limiting the square footage of a house someone can use for business purposes and thereby constraining how budding entrepreneurs can earn a living.

Throwing roadblocks in front of food trucks

Cities can be particularly hard on specific types of businesses.

The Institute for Justice report highlights the example of food trucks. While many Americans have come to embrace them for their ability to offer an array of service in a way that's both conveniently accessible and often lower cost than a traditional restaurant, cities can be quite hard on them. Often, stifling rules are a consequence of advocacy by brick-and-mortar businesses that simply don't like the competition.

In Seattle, mobile food vendors "cannot operate within 50 feet of a brick-and-mortar food service business." Likewise Phoenix, Ariz. imposes arbitrary restrictions on food truck owners, barring the managing of more than one food truck.

San Francisco is particularly onerous. Food truck operators there must fill out 16 different forms (compared to 10 in Boise), go through 44 steps from start to finish (compared to 30 in Boise) and pay an average of $3,200 in fees (compared to $684 in Boise).

But on top of that, San Francisco throws in further roadblocks. "[Any] member of the public can object to the issuance of a food truck license during a 30-day public comment period, triggering a public hearing that can significantly delay food truck owners from getting down to business," notes the IJ report.

From overly complicated processes to subjecting a food truck operator to the subjective whims of others, these examples all speak to just how silly cities can get.

"Instead of fearing innovations like food trucks, local policymakers should consider revisiting the way they regulate mobile food vending in their city," advised IJ. "Embracing the flexibility, diversity, and opportunity that food trucks provide is a win-win-win for vendors, customers, and local officials."

More broadly speaking, when it comes to licensing and permitting processes, the goal shouldn't be to bilk business owners or to limit economic competition, but to make it easy for people to set up shop and sell goods and services to people who want to buy from them.

In California, Santa Ana food truck owners complained that the Board of Equalization, a tax board, was slamming them with tax bills based on unrealistic estimates of their food sales – and then the city government harassed them with large fines for picayune violations.[3]

On a positive note, the Seattle Department of Transportation, as of this writing, is considering easing its restrictions on mobile food vendors, namely, the 50-foot buffer rule. "Some of the restrictions that we had for vending pre-pandemic didn't seem like they were necessary anymore," Alyce Nelson, public space manager for SDOT, told the local NPR affiliate.[4]

How could cities ease the rules?

The Institute for Justice's recommendations, which they developed in consultation with business owners, includes calls for cutting licensing requirements that aren't strictly necessary to protect health and safety, reducing licensing fees and creating a one-stop-shop "where applicants can access and complete all the paperwork they need … with a single sign-on."

To the latter point, it is the 21st century. City Hall websites could fulfill this purpose by having a simplified, easy-to-use portal online to achieve this task.

Some cities have opened physical "one-stop-shop" operations for certain purposes. In 2017, for example, the city of Riverside, California established a one-stop-shop, which "brings together on one floor all city departments that are part of the development process, with exclusive use of an express elevator, cell phone charging stations and a concierge-type system that helps customers obtain permits and approvals faster than ever."[5]

The same concept could be applied more broadly.

Engaging – rather than fighting – businesses

Cities can and should proactively engage the business community in a formalized way in order to identify tangible barriers to entrepreneurship and propose removing them.

The city of Aurora, Colo., established a Red Tape Reduction Committee in Dec. 2021. The committee held multiple hearings soliciting input from local businesses and private organizations, with the aim of developing ideas for how the city could make it easier to do business.[6]

The city clearly learned a few things.

"To build capacity and eliminate bottlenecks, the city is in the process of reorganizing the Public Works Department to consolidate engineering, traffic, real property, public improvements, and building staff," announced the city, which also expedited its review process for pad ready developments.[7]

Informed by the committee, the City Council eliminated certain fees and city licenses, increased the building length for multifamily buildings, reduced the city's restrictive minimum distance between liquor stores and even repealed a 65-year old ban on ice cream trucks.

What makes this example remarkable is its simplicity. Any city can do it.

The bottom line for helping businesses' bottom line

Cities need to break out of their existing regulatory schemes and start thinking how they can make it easy for people to earn a living. Sometimes that means reassessing whether permitting systems are overly complicated or not. Sometimes that means streamlining existing processes. And sometimes that means directly engaging outside of city hall for ideas.

The point should be to make it easier, not harder, for people to earn a living. Rather than viewing business as a revenue generating opportunity for city hall, city governments should view business as a critical means by which people in a city relate to and serve others.

Get City Hall out of the way of people trying to help

Rather than be a force for problem solving, City Hall can often get in the way of private, community responses and solutions to problems. To focus on one broad category where everyone agrees the government has failed: homelessness.

In August 2022, North Las Vegas authorities destroyed tiny homes for the homeless built on private property by the nonprofit New Leaf Building Community because the property was zoned for single-family homes.

A state law passed in Nevada in 2021 instructs cities to allow the construction of tiny homes, but cities have until 2024 to comply. Code enforcement officials decided it was in the best interests of the homeless to have them continue living on the streets rather than in the constructed tiny homes. "Now I sleep on the damn sidewalk because of this!" a homeless man told a local news outlet following the dismantling of the homes.[8]

As Elizabeth Nolan Brown at *Reason Magazine* points out, there's been no shortage of tiny home destructions by city governments.

In 2016, a *Los Angeles Times* headline blared, "L.A. seizes tiny houses from homeless people." As *Reason* reported, "A man named Elvis Summers had been building and giving away small wooden houses with solar lights (and American flags!) to the homeless in L.A.; the city has already confiscated three of them on freeway overpasses, and plans to snatch 7 more of them today, according to the city Bureau of Sanitation. Councilman Curren Price ordered the theft."[9]

Perhaps one could quibble with any of these particular examples. Maybe tiny home constructions need to be monitored by government officials to make sure no one is harmed. Maybe a world in which homeless people sleeping in these tiny homes would have been more dangerous and harmful than one in which those homeless people slept on the streets instead. But, on the other hand, given the failure of governments on homelessness, maybe not.

These actions by private individuals trying to help may have been haphazard, acts of compassionate desperation by people tired of waiting on the government. But city governments can and do get in the way of even more organized and professional efforts to help people.

The story of Mary's Village

Consider the story of Mary's Village in the city of San Bernardino. First opened in 2020, the 85-bed facility provides not only a place for homeless men to live, but also provides job training and other services to encourage the men to get back on their feet.

"Our goal is to give a hand-up, not a hand-out," Terry Kent, a board member of Mary's Mercy Center, Inc., which runs the facility, told the *San Bernardino Sun* in 2020. "Our goal is to take these men, educate them and help them deal with whatever problem came up in their lives. We're not here to judge, we're here to help and give them the tools to be an important part of society once again."[10]

The project, backed by a litany of sponsors, including the San Manuel Band of Mission Indians and Southern California Edison, is the sort of private sector initiative any city should welcome. The organization boasts an extensive record of operating transitional and re-entry homes for men, women and children facing challenges like homelessness and domestic violence. It also has operated food distribution, free dental and medical screening programs.[11]

Who or what could possibly stand in their way? Well, San Bernardino City Hall did. In 2016, Mary's Mercy Center sought city approval for them to build Mary's Village. What followed was a rollercoaster of indecisiveness from City Hall.

City staff recommended approval of the conditional use permit and accompanying land use adjustments to allow it to move forward. "The existing property will be transformed from a vacant underutilized site into a development that meets the city's special housing needs, while satisfying the development code requirements and will be adequately regulated through the conditions of approval in order to minimize potential impacts," the city noted.

"This project is a gift to this community, that somebody else is going to pay for," said then-City Manager Mark Scott at the city's July 18, 2016 meeting, noting the project didn't require city funding. "I can't for the life of me see how that hurts us."[12]

A majority of the City Council agreed, voting 4-2 to advance it, with opponents making generic and unsupported claims the project would attract more homeless people to the city. Then, inexplicably, just two weeks later, the council reversed itself, voting to block the project after Councilman Benito Barrios, who had voted for it the first time, switched his vote without explanation.[13]

The project was brought back to the council two months later, on Oct. 10, but a few members of the council failed to show up to the meeting and so reconsideration of the project was delayed.

The following month, the council once again approved the project, with Barrios changing his mind again, saying, cryptically, "From a compassionate side, the church is doing something to help people. But I was also told to follow the money … that's the one thing I haven't done yet. … But at this point I know a decision has to be made to do something."[14]

In December, four months after work could have started to serve a critical need in San Bernardino, the council gave its final blessings.

Grandma's House of Hope

The story of Grandma's House of Hope, based in Anaheim, Calif., is yet another instance of City Hall getting in the way arbitrarily. The nonprofit, founded by Je'Net Kreitner, who experienced homelessness herself in the 1990s, has provided emergency, transitional and bridge housing to homeless individuals since 2004.

Unlike the previous example, Grandma's House of Hope does receive public funding – its main source of funding is from the county, which contracts with the nonprofit to do what it does best.

In 2021 alone, they housed 329 people, about half of whom were victims of domestic violence or human trafficking, and most of whom suffered from mental health issues and/or had a disabling condition. Those who go through their programs are offered case management, counseling and mentorship, helping many get their lives on track.

Also in 2021, the organization proposed turning one large, two-story house on a 30,000-square-foot lot into a transitional living facility for over a dozen mentally ill homeless women. While city staff recommended a plan that called for an even larger project, the Anaheim Planning Commission buckled under pressure from nearby residents who objected to the home.

"To appease residents' concerns, [Kreitner] reduced the number of occupants from 21 to 16 (a successful graduate of Grandma's House of Hope would supervise the home overnight)," reported the *Orange County Register*. "No drinking or drugs would be allowed, the women would have a curfew, and they'd stop using the property's pool and sport courts at 9 p.m."[15]

Even so, the City Council, too, spiked the proposal, spurring a lawsuit from Grandma's House of Hope against the city.

"Nothing about the proposed shelter violates Anaheim's existing land-use regulations, and the vague and subjective nature of the complaints sure seems like a pretext to deny the shelter its permit," argued Sam Spiegelman and Jeremy Talcott, attorneys at Pacific Legal Foundation, which is representing Grandma's House of Hope, in an op-ed for the *Orange County Register*.[16]

As with the previous example, we have an instance where organizations with a proven track record of helping particularly vulnerable populations find themselves blocked not because they violated some immutable rule, but because some people simply didn't like what they were proposing.

In this case, the owner of the property, who rents out another of his properties to Grandma's House of Hope without issue, wants the proposal to be accepted.

Should there be a heckler's veto on how others use their private property? That's essentially what's happened in this instance. The use of the property is consistent with all other rules the city has in place, and yet city officials are stopping a worthy project from advancing because some people want to use the power of city hall to control the property of others.

While the courts may or may not correct this particular rejection, the ability of organized groups to leverage the city to spike activities they simply don't like, regardless of property rights or consistency with pre-established rules, is made possible by the nature of city governments.

Hence, you get outcomes like the case of NIMBYs (Not In My Back Yarders) shouting down housing for mentally ill homeless women in Anaheim. On top of that, special interests not only take advantage of the powers of city governments to stop things they don't like, but they can use the machinations of city governments to do things they want.

The special interest vulnerability of city halls

As Chapman University Law Professor Tom Bell notes in his 2018 book *Your Next Government?*, while the average city consists of many thousands of people cumulatively owning vast proportions of a city — from residential to commercial to industries properties — no one truly owns a city in the way one owns one's home.

"Instead of owners, cities rely on hired professionals and civically minded volunteers to protect their assets from unrestrained exploitation," notes Bell. "Those devices seem fated to always permit a great deal of nibbling around the edges, however, and they often allow special interests to consume great chunks of the public good."[17]

Consider the following examples of cities being led astray by special interest considerations. One is a story involving big business, the other, big labor.

Anaheim's incoherence

On occasion, city leaders are able to resist the temptation to indulge special interests, focus on their core functions and explicitly embrace deregulation and the importance of encouraging private sector activity.

One (fleeting) example of this is the experience of the city of Anaheim a decade ago when, under the leadership of Councilman and then Mayor Tom Tait, the city championed a "freedom culture" which focused on facilitating investment and development in the city. Rather than doling out subsidies or creating new city bureaucracies, the city moved to streamline development and simplify its permitting processes to spur economic growth.[18]

"While the state and other cities may continue to add burdens to business owners, Anaheim's freedom and kindness agenda mandates a different approach," explained the 2011 report of the city's Regulatory Relief Task Force. "Regulatory barriers interfere with the ability of citizens in Anaheim to pursue their economic dreams by increasing costs, imposing delays, and introducing risk and uncertainty when launching, expanding, and operating local businesses."[19]

However, this attitude soon gave way to crony capitalism amid heavy political campaign spending by Walt Disney Corp. to steer the city in a pro-subsidy direction. Rather than facilitating private investment by getting out of the way, politically captured city leaders embraced the notion of using the power of government to dole out subsidies.

A 20-year, $267 million hotel subsidy so Disney could build a four-diamond hotel was eventually approved by the city. But this in turn ignited public backlash, prompted a union push to require businesses which received subsidies to pay higher minimum wages and ultimately resulted in Disney walking away from the subsidy.[20]

If that sounds like a convoluted mess, that's because it is. The city's turn to cronyism created factions where factions shouldn't have existed and turned Anaheim City Hall into a proxy for special interest battles over how to use city government for their own benefit.

Santa Ana's approach to fees

Then there's the recent experience of the city of Santa Ana, California, with housing developer fees. From 2015 to 2020, the city required housing developers who did not plan for "affordable housing" units in their proposed housing developments to pay in-lieu fees of $15 per square foot to the city so the city could fund "affordable" units elsewhere.[21]

The result was predictable.

"No developers pulled building permits from October 2015 [until] September 2020, when we reduced the fees to $5 per square foot, along with other items," Councilman Phil Bacerra reminded his colleagues in 2022. "That was zero dollars going towards down payment assistance for first-time homebuyers. That's zero dollars going towards rehabbing existing affordable units here in Santa Ana."[22]

In a rational world, Santa Ana city officials would have learned that rather than stifling the ability of developers to build needed housing in their city, they should learn from past mistakes and avoid imposing mandates that deter developers from building homes in their city.

But this is the real world, where political considerations come into play. Councilman Bacerra had to remind his colleagues of the city's experience with imposing costly mandates on developers from 2015 to 2020 because they came up with yet another convoluted scheme to impose new mandates on developers.

On April 19, 2022, the council voted to bring back the $15 per square foot in-lieu fee. Under the plan, developers could get some relief from the higher in-lieu fee so long as a certain proportion of the labor used in the development is union labor. In either case, developers will be forced to either pay more to build or to decide not to pull permits, as they chose for five years the last time.

"Although state law in effect requires union labor for public works projects, such as highways, privately financed projects are exempt," explained Dan Walters in a column for *CalMatters*.

"The new Santa Ana ordinance is part of a concerted effort by construction unions to extend the requirement to private developments either by law or local ordinance."[23]

In other words, instead of working with developers to figure out how to make it easier and cheaper to build needed housing, Santa Ana officials decided to do the bidding of politically influential construction unions and make it more expensive to build housing in their city even if it jeopardizes their ability to build more homes and collect in-lieu fees.

"This is something that hopefully other communities will emulate," Mayor Vicente Sarmiento said in defense of the ordinance when passed.[24] Only time will tell how long it will take Santa Ana city officials to walk back the fee hike this time.

City services are subject to political pressures and distortions

As with rule-making and overall governance, government provided services can be subject to political considerations rather than practical or customer-oriented considerations.

"The consumer of food and the consumer of clothing have a tremendous variety from which to choose; not so the consumer of police protection or garbage collection or ambulance service at least in most cities where these services are government monopolies," noted Robert Poole in his 1980 book *Cutting Back City Hall.*[25]

Unlike the immediate response mechanisms one can exercise with the private sector – one can stop buying from one store and go to another – the ordinary person has very little recourse when city services aren't very good.

"Voting once every few years for city council members gives a citizen very little impact on the type and quality of public services provided," he continued. "Yet the same citizen's daily vote at the supermarket, with each purchase, can determine the fate, not only of Swift and Del Monte, but of Safeway and A&P as well."[26]

To Poole's point, city governments can and do offer a wide array of services to the public, sometimes well, sometimes not, sometimes cost-effectively, sometimes not.

Some services are viewed as core functions of local governments, like policing, though cities will sometimes contract with larger law enforcement entities like sheriffs' departments to avoid having to manage a local police department and to ideally benefit from economies of scale.

Other services, like waste management, will either be provided directly by city employees, contracted by a city to a private company, or left completely to residents or homeowners associations to sort out. How and how well cities provide these services can make the difference between having a competently run public safety system or not, well-maintained roads or not, and so on.

Oftentimes, a major determinant of this can be the extent to which public employee unions become the central beneficiary of municipal service delivery. The unionization rate for public employees nationwide is five times higher than in the private sector and they have clearly made that work for themselves.

"In 2019, California state government workers earned an average of $143,000 per year [in total compensation], while local government employees earned nearly as much, averaging about $131,000 annually," noted UCLA professor Lee Ohanian. "But

California's private sector workers earned about $71,000, roughly half as much as their public sector counterparts."[27]

This pattern plays out beyond California as well. In 2018, the Nevada Policy Research Institute found, "The median annual earnings for local government workers in [Nevada] was $58,644 – 46 percent higher than the $40,259 received by private-sector employees. That's the largest disparity nationwide and more than six times that of the 8 percent differential for the median state."[28]

While some of this may be explainable by, say, differences in types of work, relative average education levels and so on, it's apparent public employee unions have a particular incentive to keep government services going for reasons that don't necessarily have to do with getting things done for the taxpaying public.

As will be discussed further, public employee unions routinely lead the charge in shutting down any talk of providing services differently. They have their own turf to protect.

This distorts the purpose of city services and, also, directly and indirectly impacts the economic dynamics of a city. Failures of governments to limit public expenditures responsibly will often force them to choose either cuts to services or tax increases or both.

Either way, that means city residents get left holding the bag, ceding money that could've been used more productively in the private sector to City Halls delivering them fewer and lesser services.

Los Angeles, or, how not to run a city

The city of Los Angeles has a lot going for it. It's the ultimate melting pot, uniting people with backgrounds from all over the world. But the city government is a mess and it's an embodiment of all of the problems written so far.

In December 2013, Los Angeles civic leaders, organized as the "Los Angeles 2020 Commission," published a blunt assessment of the state of Los Angeles. Titled, "A Time For Truth," the report warned the city risked becoming "a city in decline."[29] Sadly, many of the words written then remain true today.

The city at the time suffered from poor assessments of business friendliness – the report called the city's permitting processes "daunting" and referenced the "long and arduous" process of complying with city regulations.

The result of this was a situation where a city which should have many advantages – an international reputation, world-class universities, nationally important ports and of course no shortage of people – ended up with a high rate of poverty and a high rate of low-wage work replacing higher wage work.[30]

Today, little has changed on either front. Los Angeles continues to have a high rate of poverty.[31] There's also been ongoing economic bifurcation. From 2009 to 2018, according to the Los Angeles County Economic Development Corporation, among the 10 occupational categories which saw the greatest increase in Los Angeles County, half paid well below $30,000 per year (in a county with a median income of around $40,000) and three of the rest paid two to three times the median income level.[32]

The 2020 Commission also expressed concern about the city's "poor planning and outdated zoning," which made the development decision "subject to the whims of special interests, NIMBYism and City Hall insiders."

In the years since then, Los Angeles has been rocked by corruption scandals involving the city's control over land-use decisions.

"Corruption has again been exposed at Los Angeles City Hall, with one council member under indictment in a development scandal and another having pleaded guilty to his part in it," wrote L.A's former deputy mayor Rick Cole, former planning direct Gail Goldberg and former deputy mayor and general manager Bud Ovrom, in a 2020 *Los Angeles Times* column. "The transgressions highlight the real-world consequences of failing to modernize outdated planning codes and leaving decision-making power over development projects in the hands of City Council members."[33]

Due to the city's failure to write clear and easy-to-follow rules they thereby fostered a situation where corruption was bound to occur. Instead of merely writing land-use policies that developers could reasonably abide by, they left in place outdated rules requiring developers to beg City Council members for help.

Perhaps unsurprisingly given these dynamics, in 2020 Councilman José Huizar, head of the planning and land use management committee, was indicted for allegedly taking bribes from Chinese developers. Councilman Mitch Englander, also a member of the committee, pleaded guilty to corruption charges in a separate case.[34]

In another perennial issue for the city, the 2020 report also decried rising pension costs. "Pension costs accounted for 3% of the city's budget a decade ago and 18% this year," it noted. "The cost of covering further increases will cut into the city's ability to supply services."

According to a report written by former Assemblyman Joe Nation for the Stanford Institute for Economic Policy Research, while the city contributed $343 million toward pensions in 2003-04, by 2017-18, the city was on the hook for $1.4 billion in annual contributions.[35]

Step back and think about that. While the city's pension obligations have begun to stabilize and may have finally begun their long descent, increasing proportions of the city's budget went not to services – but to pay for the retirements of city employees.

This phenomenon of "pension crowd-out" is happening across the country, but it's especially acute in cities like Los Angeles where public employee unions carry considerable influence. Instead of ensuring that the roads have been paved or the homeless are housed, huge sums of money have been going to retired city workers who retire at surprisingly early ages.

And, finally, consider the homeless problem for which Los Angeles is well known. "Los Angeles is called the capital of the homeless for good reason," the 2020 Commission report said nine years ago. Today, there are over 41,290 homeless people in the city of Los Angeles. The city's failure on homelessness has been nothing short of a scandal.

In 2016, Los Angeles leaders pitched and city voters approved Measure HHH, which raised $1.2 billion in funds to build homes for homeless people. Developers supported passage of the bond. What could go wrong?

Well, there was a 45 percent increase in the city's homeless population in the five years following Measure HHH's passage, thousands of homeless people died over that period and there was an inadequate number of slowly built, increasingly expensive housing units funded by the measure.

"For projects in construction, the average per-unit cost increased from $531,000 in 2020 to $596,846 in 2021," reported City Controller Ron Galperin in a 2022 letter to city leaders. "Fourteen percent of the units in construction exceed $700,000 per unit, and one project in pre-development is estimated to cost almost $837,000 per unit, $100,000 more per unit than the most expensive project in 2020."[36]

This is what happens when you hand a dysfunctional, special interest-captured city government over a billion dollars. Rather than swiftly and cost-effectively help the homeless, city officials made sure developers helped themselves.

"Politicians measure success by how much money they have raised to combat homelessness. Service providers with clipboards endlessly approach homeless individuals with services and promises to return, yet are unable to provide sufficient shelter or housing. Bureaucrats create statistics trumpeting their efficiency and success to the public. But none of this has led to accountability or solutions," wrote federal Judge David Carter in a scathing 2021 ruling condemning the city of Los Angeles' failures on homelessness.[37]

LA's brief flirtation with doing things differently

"Why do we have to own a zoo?" wondered then-Los Angeles Mayor Antonio Villaraigosa in a March 2009 meeting with writers at the *Los Angeles Business Journal*. "A lot of cities don't own their own zoos; they are privately run or have a public-private partnership structure. And, while we're at it, why do we have to own a convention center?"[38]

Fiscal crises tend to focus the minds of politicians and force city officials to reconsider what it is that they really need to be doing. "We were looking at bankruptcy and I had to make a lot of tough calls," recalled Villaraigosa in an interview. "Things I might not have done otherwise I had to do."[39]

The context of these questions raised by Villaraigosa in 2009, of course, was the Great Recession. At the time, the city of Los Angeles was forecasting consecutive annual budget shortfalls of $450 million to $500 million per year.[40]

In December 2008, a report commissioned by then-City Controller Laura Chick recommended the city privatize dozens of services, including city-owned golf courses and parking facilities, Ontario International Airport, solid waste collection and operation of the Hyperion Waste Water Treatment facility.[41]

"The cost of delivering essential services keeps growing at a rate that exceeds the city's ability to generate revenue, and is a major reason we've had a structural deficit for years now," Chick wrote in a letter to Villaraigosa. "When it comes to looking at how the city can fulfill its obligations to the public, and pay for it, no subject should be taboo."[42]

In the years that followed, the Los Angeles City Council would go on to hand over operations of the city's convention center to the Anschutz Entertainment Group. "I believed the private sector would be a better steward of the convention center," recalls Villaraigosa.[43]

He was right. Just a few years after operations of the convention center were turned over to private hands, the AEG boasted of "an operating surplus year after year, a healthy reserve of $7.1 million, reinvesting more than $40 million in building improvement and alteration projects, increasing citywide conventions, and the reimbursement of $7.7 million to the city of Los Angeles for the Department of Convention & Tourism Development (CTD) overhead since privatization," according to a convention center statement.[44]

Unfortunately, the same couldn't happen for many other city functions which weren't privatized, including the city zoo. Though there were negotiations between the city and the Greater Los Angeles Zoo Association, those negotiations broke down when the city sought more control over the zoo than the nonprofit thought was justified or workable.

"The zoo association, with the backing of Mayor Antonio Villaraigosa, had long pushed privatizing zoo operations as a way to stave off annual budget cuts that have increasingly chipped away at the zoo's operations," reported *Los Angeles Business Journal* in 2012. "A private operator, they argued, would have more freedom to market the zoo and increase visitor traffic."[45]

Indeed, Villaraigosa to this day cites the San Diego Zoo as an example of a well-run and well-regarded zoo that isn't run by a city government. It's one of the biggest zoos in the world, home to over 4,000 animals and draws people from all over the world. Part of the zoo's success is that it is owned and operated by the San Diego Zoo Wildlife Alliance, a nonprofit organization.

Most zoos, in fact, aren't managed by government agencies.

"According to a recent study of the Association of Zoos and Aquariums, more than 80 percent of its accredited zoos throughout the world are non-government managed and largely operated by not-for-profit entities," noted Los Angeles City Controller Ron Galperin in a 2018 report calling on the city to revisit the governing structure of the zoo.[46]

Galperin's report, citing a 2003 article "Characteristics of a world-class zoo or aquarium in the 21st century" published by the Zoological Society of London, noted that "government administrative bureaucracy can be stifling and government-run zoos may find it difficult to become 'world-class.'"[47]

That's because zoos and aquariums "need the flexibility to: 1) recruit and hire the best personnel; 2) remove unproductive personnel more easily; 3) speed up decision-making processes; 4) take more risks; and, 5) be less subject to the vagaries of government funding and political cycles."[48]

Yes, fill in your own joke here, we are in fact still talking only about zoos and aquariums.

Galperin's report makes a point of acknowledging that handing over operations of significant cultural institutions in Los Angeles over to the private sector is hardly new. Los Angeles County handed over operations of the Los Angeles County Museum of Art, Natural History Museum and the Music Center to nonprofit organizations. They are doing just fine, fulfilling their civic missions.[49]

In a joint letter to Galperin, the general manager of the zoo and the president of the nonprofit Greater Los Angeles Zoo Association (GLAZA) likewise pointed out the successful privatization of the Dallas Zoo in 2009.

"Attendance at the Dallas Zoo set records in the years following the governance transition; zoo visitorship increased by a quarter of a million people in the first three years and reached

1,000,000 attendees in 2016 for the first time in the zoo's 128-year history," they wrote. "Revenues have grown as well, increasing from a loss of $1.4 million at the time of privatization to a surplus of $364,000 in three years."[50]

As tends to happen with government reports, Galperin's report sits on the city controller website and the LA Zoo remains subject to city ownership and operation.

The enduring logic of privatization

"Virtually every category [of public services] has been or is being provided by a private organization somewhere in the United States: police, fire, paramedics, roads, water parks, recreation, garbage – even tax assessment," noted Poole in *Cutting Back City Hall.*[51]

It was true four decades ago when he wrote those words and it's true now: Much of what city governments do can, is done by or should be reliably done by the private sector. While times and contexts change, the underlying principles of privatization remain the same.

"Private firms tend to be efficient precisely because they have to make a profit," explained Poole. "A municipal agency, for instance, has permanent, guaranteed access to tax funds and a guaranteed monopoly on the service. There is little incentive for it to be efficient and save money. A private firm, on the other hand, has no long-term guarantee of funds."[52]

There are obvious political reasons for government officials to want to keep services in-house and done by government employees.

Public employee unions, for self-evidently rational reasons on their part, don't like the idea of being put out of business and have clear incentives to ensure the election and re-election of council members who not only won't raise matters of privatization (or outsourcing) but who would vigorously oppose the idea if it ever came up.

But from the perspective of an ordinary person, who isn't a city government employee and couldn't distinguish between a government-employee and a private sector-employee, what should matter is whether the same task can be performed as well or even better.

"When the cost of outsourcing is less or the same, and the service quality is the same or better than the corresponding government workforce can provide on its own, it makes sense to contract out," suggests Austill Stuart, director of privatization and government reform at the Reason Foundation, which Robert Poole co-founded. "The important thing is to ensure those costs and benefits are properly determined to make an informed decision."[53]

One condition that helps ensure that is if there's competition – when there are multiple private sector service providers available to take on a project, that can help cities discern good quality operators from lesser ones.

Principles of privatization

Cities will routinely contract either management of services or the direct delivery of services to private companies. As in the previously discussed case of Los Angeles, times of fiscal challenges are a common time for privatization to be on the table.

To take a simple example, the outsourcing of trash collection services is quite common. According to a 2020 report by consulting firm R3, out of more than 500 cities in the state of California, there are just 50 city-operated waste management operations.[54]

In 2016, as part of its bankruptcy exit plan, the city of San Bernardino agreed to outsource trash and related services to a private company, Burrtec. Under the agreement, all 58 of the city's full-time public employees were offered full-time positions. In exchange for taking on the responsibility of handling trash collection, Burrtec agreed to pay the city tens of millions of dollars.[55]

Without the pressure of a bankruptcy, though, public employee unions can rally to shut down such considerations.

In 2020, just before the pandemic, amid talk the city could face insolvency in the years ahead, the city of Riverside, Calif., considered doing the same. Even though a city-commissioned report indicated the city could save money by contracting out trash collection unions ensured the matter was rejected and the proposal was spiked 5-2 by the council.[56]

To take another simple example, golf courses. For many cities, they're a bit of an unusual asset for a city to own and operate because they tend to serve only a sliver of city residents. They're often costly to maintain. One can imagine other uses for such sprawling land. And, of course, there's no shortage of completely private golf courses. When there's a private sector correlate, that might be regarded as a strong signal privatization or outsourcing are the way to go.

To manage costs, some cities outsource operations of golf courses. Marc Joffe, a policy analyst at the Reason Foundation, notes, "Antioch, California, for example, contracts out the operation of its municipal golf course to a private company. Antioch Public Golf Course, Inc. has been operating the city's Lone Tree Golf Course since 1982 and has the concessions contract through 2033."[57]

In 2014, the city of Phoenix, amid a growing budget deficit running its municipal golf courses, approved a 30-year lease of the formerly named Maryvale Municipal Golf Course, handing over operations to the private Grand Canyon University. "The new private managers took on all operating costs and invested $8 million for course repairs and an upgraded clubhouse, and it will pay the city of Phoenix 10% of net revenues after it recoups its upfront investment," noted Adrian Moore, vice president of policy at the Reason Foundation. This arrangement worked so well Phoenix went on to privatize six other city-owned golf courses."[58]

Phoenix's experience helped reinforce calls by the free market Rio Grande Foundation in New Mexico to call for the city of Albuquerque to either privatize or sell city golf courses. From 2012 to 2016, city golf courses saw expenses grow from $3.9 million to $5.1 million even as revenues declined from $3.8 million to $3.5 million over that same period. "[W]hy does the city own golf courses at all?" asked the group in a 2017 policy brief.[59] Indeed.

In the specific instance of golf courses, Joffe likely has it right when he argues, "Ideally, local governments should be looking to sell this valuable real estate they are sitting on to pay down unfunded public pension liabilities, fund needed infrastructure repairs and expansions, and maximize the value for taxpayers rather than losing money on golf."[60]

Maybe waste management and golf courses are fairly simple. There are even more complicated (and often expensive) city services that the private sector can handle.

De-bureaucratizing airports

I fly often through Los Angeles International Airport and I'm always left wondering, Why do governments need to own airports? Is there any particular reason the city of Los Angeles needs to own LAX?

The answer to the latter question is no. The rest of the world is actually far ahead of the United States in realizing this and letting the private sector handle the business of owning and operating airports. According to Airports Council International Europe, 21 percent of European airports are fully privatized and another 31 percent have a mix of public and private shareholders.[61]

"During the pandemic, new privately-owned or operated airports were also opened or announced in Chile, Bulgaria, India and Guinea," reported Peter Shawn Taylor in *C2C Journal* in 2022. "And this past April Brazil sold 22 small regional airports in a heated auction that earned substantially more than the government had been expecting."[62]

Today, there is only one privatized airport in the United States – and it's not in a state. It's Luis Muñoz Marín International Airport in San Juan, Puerto Rico. The deal proved lucrative for Puerto Rico, which entailed significant upfront and ongoing revenue to the commonwealth.

"Aerostar Airport Holdings paid $615 million in upfront proceeds to the Puerto Rico Ports Authority, and will pay a further estimated $550 million over the 40-year lease that includes an annual lease payment of $2.5 million for the first five years of the contract, 5% of gross airport revenues during the following 25 years, and 10% of gross airport revenues during the final 10 years of the lease," reported the Congressional Research Service in 2021.[63]

Part of the holdup for the United States is that Congress only recently opened the door to privatized airports. "In the United States, privatization was legalized for a limited number of airports in 1997, and in 2018, Congress opened privatization to any U.S. airport," noted Joseph Guinto in a 2020 piece for *The Atlantic*.[64]

Rather than leaving such major transportation systems in the hands of governments, particularly local governments with all the frailties discussed in this booklet, it's time to give privatized airports a chance.

"Airports should be self-funded by revenues from passengers, airlines, concessions, and other sources," argued Robert Poole and Chris Edwards in 2016. "Federal subsidies should be phased out, and state and local governments should privatize their airports to improve efficiency, competitiveness, and passenger benefits."[65]

Freeing fire and emergency medical services

This needs to be said. When most of the people in a given field are volunteers, and most of the actual tasks of people in a line of work can be done by the private sector, one could be forgiven for wondering why it's a major expenditure for city governments.

In this case, I'm talking about firefighting. According to the National Fire Protection Association, about 67 percent of America's firefighters are volunteers.[66] Municipal fire departments operated mainly with volunteers also exist – including in Blythe, Calif.

For most fire departments, medical calls make up the vast majority of calls for service. According to NFPA, of the 34 million calls to fire departments nationwide in 2019, 24.5 million were for medical aid or rescue calls. In fact, there are more "false alarm" calls (2.9 million) than calls for fires (1.3 million).[67]

Given the reorientation of fire departments, particularly in larger jurisdictions, toward providing emergency medical services (EMS) in conjunction with fire services, it's worth rethinking whether the model of costly fire departments as they commonly exist makes sense. After all, the private sector has both historically handled and currently handles EMS services in many jurisdictions.

For now, however, with the considerable influence of both fire departments and especially unions representing fire department employees, this is a conversation that needs to be had.

Truly private firefighting

Founded in 1948, Rural Metro Fire is a private, for-profit fire department serving communities throughout the country.

The company was founded by a newspaperman, Louis Witzeman, who lived in an unincorporated part of what's now Scottsdale and took it upon himself to provide fire services in his area after witnessing a house fire that wasn't responded to by the local municipal fire department because it was beyond their jurisdiction.

"There was no fire protection for his home, and he simply wanted to get it. Neighbors promised to pay him $10 a year for fire protection, and the 21-year-old Witzeman invested his last $900 in a fire truck," explained Nancy Poole in a 1991 article for the Foundation for Economic Education. "Stuck with the truck when his neighbors didn't follow through, Witzeman had to go into business. So it was that one truck, four men, and a modest budget started a fire protection subscription-based business that grossed $30,000 in its first year."[68]

Today, Rural Metro Fire, which merged with ambulance company American Medical Response, is contracted by localities, fire districts, private insurance companies and individual homeowners to provide fire services in states across the country.

Consistent with its founding, Rural Metro Fire continues to service homes in unincorporated areas beyond the scope of municipal government departments, particularly in Arizona but also Oregon and Tennessee.[69]

Robert Poole notes that, for a time in the 1980s, the notion of private firefighting services gained a fair bit of momentum, so much so that "a small contract fire-service industry emerged in the 1980s and had its own trade association — the Private Sector Fire Association."[70]

He continues, "The national firefighters union saw this development, including a number of small cities that switched from in-house to contract fire service — as a major threat. They worked very hard, politically, to defeat early conversions," such as in Hall County, Ga., "by organizing recalls of the elected officials who had brought about the shift. Within a few years, such contracts pretty much dried up and the Private Sector Fire Association was disbanded."[71]

One practical consequence of the Private Sector Fire Association's disbanding is that there aren't enough service providers – unlike in the case of waste management where, in addition to Burrtec, there are many other well-established private companies providing the service – to make it a feasible option to discuss anymore.

But, you never know what the private sector is capable of.

Placentia scraps government EMS services, draws wrath of fire unions

Here's a more recent example of how aggressive government firefighting service providers can be in protecting their turf.

In the 1970s, the city of Placentia in Orange County, California, disbanded its city-run fire department in favor of contracting with the Orange County Fire Authority. While economies of scale served the city well, rising costs, particularly pension obligations, forced city officials to reconsider contracting with the county.[72]

Between 2009 and 2018, the city reported costs with OCFA grew 54 percent "with no change in service levels." Over that same time period, the city's revenues increased only 10 percent.

In 2009, while just 26.18 percent of the city's public safety budget went toward the OCFA contract, Placentia projected that by 2029, 47.47 percent of the city's budget would go toward that contract. The elephant in the room, of course, was that most of what the county's fire services consisted of wasn't firefighting but emergency medical services. A 2022 report from the Orange County Grand Jury notes that, "nearly 80 percent of all 911 calls to fire departments are for medical services."[73]

Logically, then, Placentia proposed forming its own fire department – offering competitive pay and defined contribution retirement options instead of defined benefit pensions – and contracting with a private company to provide EMS services.

This disentangling of fire and emergency medical services is quite common across the country and in California it was the norm prior to the 1970s. However, amid reduced calls for fire services thanks to enforcement of modern building codes and fire prevention systems, "fire departments broadened their service models and capabilities, creating an all-hazards approach to emergency services delivery."[74]

While this offered benefits to professional fire departments, the model is likely outdated and more conducive to delivering money to the pockets of department employees than it is offering optimal fire and EMS services, as Placentia realized.

The backlash to Placentia's proposal was swift, from both the state firefighters' union and local fire officials.

California Professional Firefighters President Brian Rice condemned the proposal, saying the city would endanger public safety by hiring "inexperienced" paramedics and firefighters.

"You guys are in a bad spot," Rice told the City Council. "Your consultants are selling snake oil … you can't get more for less."[75]

City officials also reported alleged misconduct by OCFA in retaliation.

"Placentia Police Lt. James McElhinney detailed a June 6 incident when he said an unnamed Fire Authority captain refused to let OCFA paramedics use a Lynch Ambulance vehicle to transport a patient from an assisted care facility in Yorba Linda to St. Jude's Hospital in Fullerton," reported *Voice of OC*. "He said the Fire Authority delayed transporting the victim for an unknown amount of time in order to use Fire Authority's contract ambulance provider."[76]

These experiences and more understandably troubled Placentia city officials. "Since we made the decision to change business models, we have been subjected to the most draconian negativity by fire union personnel I ever could have imagined," Councilman Paul Green said. "One could think the era of Jimmy Hoffa has returned."[77]

With the support of the state firefighters union, the California Legislature also moved to block other cities from following Placentia's lead on the pension reform side.

In 2020, union ally then-Assemblyman Patrick O'Donnell, D-Long Beach, introduced Assembly Bill 2967. The law prevents cities participating with the California Public Employees' Retirement System from concurrently offering a non-CalPERS retirement option while participating in CalPERS for other employees.[78]

The bill faced some opposition from local government groups like the League of California Cities, which argued, "[a]t a time when governments at all levels of society are struggling with the dual challenges of lowered revenues and consistent or higher demands of services, now is not the time to reduce one of the 'tools in the toolbox' for local governments to manage their operations."

However, the influence of pension giant CalPERS, which didn't like the idea of local governments getting out from under it, coupled with the political leverage of public employee unions was enough to sway all but a few lawmakers. The bill easily passed the state Assembly and state Senate, with bipartisan support, barring cities from following Placentia's lead on part of their reform effort.

However, the results of Placentia's contentious break from OCFA speak for themselves.

The city estimates it will save $3 million per year thanks to the change. Over time, these practical adjustments will free many millions of dollars for other, more beneficial purposes, mitigate the need for higher taxes and allow greater budget flexibility in difficult times. Additionally, by contracting with a private EMS company, Placentia will not only be able to achieve cost-savings but also won't have to juggle obligations toward additional public employees.

Contrary to the fear mongering of union leader Brian Rice, it didn't take long for it to be proven that, in fact, private EMS providers can do just as good a job as those tied to OCFA and can yield tangible benefits to the city.

"Using a private EMS provider with an existing infrastructure provides for an extensive surge capacity in Placentia for multi-casualty incidents and other large-scale emergencies," wrote Luis Estevez, deputy city administrator of Placentia in a commentary for the International City Managers' Association. "This resilience in our service model was proven in October 2020, as two separate wildfires burned in North Orange County at the same time. We watched in real-time as fire suppression units were being sent by our neighboring agencies from far away distances to respond to medical emergencies because the fire suppression units who would ordinarily be dispatched to those medical calls were occupied working the fire lines."[79]

The OC grand jury report recommending that fire agencies stop sending fire trucks with EMS vehicles likewise praised Placentia's alternative approach to providing firefighting and EMS services and highlighted improved response times and reduced costs.

"Preliminary statistics show that not only have city costs gone down, the time to appear on site for an EMS call also has been reduced by four minutes, from 9.5 to 5.5 [minutes]," the grand jury noted, further adding, "Placentia should receive credit for attempting (and in many ways delivering) a new and better approach to EMS."

Learning from libraries

In 1997, amid financial difficulties, Riverside County, California, handed over operations of its library system to Library Systems & Services, a private company based out of Maryland.

"We ended up privatizing, and it's been one of the better decisions this board has made in the last two decades," Supervisor John Tavaglione told the *Riverside Press-Enterprise* in 2011.[80]

Today, LS&S boasts of saving Riverside County taxpayers $900,000 per year in operational costs while increasing library hours, scheduled community events and circulation. Subsequent to Riverside County's successful contracting with LS&S, other jurisdictions followed suit, including in Los Angeles, Ventura and Shasta Counties.[81]

This naturally angered the Service Employees International Union, which in 2011 backed legislation from then-Assemblyman Das Williams, D-Santa Barbara, to discourage localities from turning over management of libraries to private providers.

In its original form, Assembly Bill 438 would have required local governments to get voter approval for plans to break from the standard county-run library systems and contract with the private sector.

SEIU peddled predictable talking points about the threat posed by "attaching a profit margin to library services." But local governments which actually went through with handing over operations to private entities experienced something not-so-sinister.[82]

"Without the ability to contract for library services, Riverside County's libraries would not be as good as they are and would certainly cost a lot more to operate," Supervisor Tavaglione wrote to his colleagues urging them to join him in opposing AB 438.[83]

The League of California Cities likewise pushed back, arguing, "Tying the hands of local government does not help a city retain services, and instead makes it significantly harder to continue to provide basic community services."[84]

45

AB 438 was eventually amended to remove the voter-approval requirement, but still imposed various cumbersome restrictions on localities considering contracting out library services. "The contract shall not be approved solely on the basis that savings will result from lower contractor pay rates or benefits," reads one of the restrictions.[85]

The bill was passed by the Legislature and signed into law by then-Gov. Jerry Brown.

Now, to be sure, LS&S still operates in communities across California and across the United States. And it must be said that LS&S, while often being contracted over long periods of time, as in Riverside County, some jurisdictions do sometimes decide they're better off returning to traditional, government-managed libraries.

Santa Clarita, California, for instance, recently ended its contract with LS&S after deciding it would be more cost-effective to in-source library management services. One way to interpret this is that privatization and contracting isn't necessarily the solution to everything. Another is that, while that may be true, the ability to swap out service providers – as one may do frequently in the private sector – is a benefit of contracting out.[86] Anyway, there's no harm in having competition.

Reason's Austill Stuart further notes that, for one thing, "only one private firm exists in the space...so it isn't very competitive," and secondly, "many decisions to have outsource public libraries were based on branches being abandoned by larger library systems, meaning smaller towns and cities would find themselves needing to operate a library without having done so before, so they contract out under duress."[87]

When contracting cuts against the public

While the private sector is often superior to the public sector, the private sector isn't immune to failings. Some efforts to contract with the private sector simply don't work out or cause greater problems. Sometimes that's a consequence of a poorly written contract, sometimes a service provider just isn't good.

But sometimes, contracted private entities do things that lead to not-so-desirable outcomes.

In 2018, for example, the cities of Coachella and Indio in Riverside County, Calif., were the subject of lawsuits over their contracts with Silver & Wright LLP to help handle nuisance complaints. The private law firm was indeed effective at what it did, and lived up to its promise to collect 100 percent of cities' costs in enforcing their municipal codes.

"The business model here of for-profit prosecution is premised on recovering fees from every criminal defendant. That creates perverse incentives, and it distorts the way prosecutors exercise their discretion," said Jeffrey Redfern, an attorney with the Institute for Justice, to NPR at the time.[88]

Stories began to emerge of people hit with massive bills.

There was the story of Ramona Morales, who ran afoul of city ordinances because tenants in one of her properties owned chickens. She also didn't have a business license. After the chickens were removed, Morales went to court to pay the $225 in fines. But upon arrival, she learned she was being criminally prosecuted over the chickens. She promptly pleaded guilty and thought that settled matters. But then Silver & Wright LLP moved to collect $6,000 in fees.[89]

Other stories included that of a Coachella man who added a new room to his house without first obtaining a permit. Beyond the expected $900 fine, he was also hit with legal bills of over $31,000. Naturally, these sorts of stories drew public outrage and even prompted legislation barring cities from engaging in such aggressive cost recovery.

Morales and the Institute for Justice ultimately filed suit and in 2018 settled with the city. Coachella followed suit.[90]

While the practice of outsourcing legal services can and often does certainly still make sense, the sort of tasks need to be carefully managed to avoid leveraging the private sector to bilk as much money out of people as possible.

Alternative government models

Cities don't need to have a cookie-cutter structure of governance. They can and do vary significantly in how they're structured and what the balance is between their role as service provider versus service broker.

The Lakewood Plan

Less radical now, and less deliberately private-sector minded, the city of Lakewood, California, pioneered the notion of a contract city with its Lakewood Plan in 1954. The city was incorporated amid an effort by the nearby city of Long Beach to take over the unincorporated area.

"Then along came John Sanford Todd, a struggling attorney and proud Lakewood resident, who dreamed up a way to preserve his community's independence without it going broke: It would become a new kind of city, one that contracted out for police protection, trash collection, firefighting – just about every service a city provides," noted the *Los Angeles Times* in a 2008 piece upon Todd's passing.[91]

Today, the city remains proud of its history and the example it set for cities across California. "Lakewood – along with about 25 percent of all California cities – has made contracting the core of its municipal operations," the city notes on its website. "These cities – also called Lakewood Plan cities – provide most of their municipal services through contracts with county agencies and private industry."[92]

Today, the city contracts out functions like trash collection and street sweeping to the private sector, while contracting with the county for law enforcement services.

Contract cities in California, which advocate and defend their respective model of governance through the California Contract Cities Association, recognize the value and flexibility that comes with being able to contract out services as needed. Having the option to contract out can help them control costs and deliver better services.

The Sandy Springs experiment

So far, what we've been discussing are your standard, run-of-the-mill cities which can and do contract out certain, particular services to the private sector. What would happen if a city contracted out nearly everything to the private sector? Well, for a little over a decade, Sandy Springs, Ga., served as an example of what that could look like.

In 2005, the city of Sandy Springs was incorporated with a population of 85,000 people making it the seventh largest city in the state. What made the new city notable was its deliberate approach of contracting out as many city services as possible.

"We have harnessed the energy of the private sector to organize the major functions of city government instead of assembling our own bureaucracy," Mayor Eva Galambos said early in the city's founding. "This we have done because we are convinced that the competitive model is what has made America so successful. And we are here to demonstrate that this same competitive model will lead to an efficient and effective local government."[93]

Though it always maintained its own police and fire departments (insurance costs of making them private made privatization cost-prohibitive), and the encompassing Fulton County continued to have responsibility for other functions (like wastewater management), Sandy Springs contracted out every other function.

Initially, the city contracted with the Colorado-based CH2M Hill, an environmental engineering company, to manage and provide other city services. But after five years, the city decided it was better off contracting services with multiple companies instead of just one to provide services ranging from right-of-way maintenance to information services to managing parks and recreation.

In a 2012 profile of how the city functioned, the *New York Times* characterized it this way: "Applying for a business license? Speak to a woman with Severn Trent, a multinational company based in Coventry, England. Want to build a new deck on your house? Chat with an employee of Collaborative Consulting, based in Burlington, Mass. Need a word with people who oversee trash collection? That would be the URS Corporation, based in San Francisco."[94]

Administrative functions at the city's court were likewise contracted out to the Pasadena, California-based Jacobs Engineering Group. And while police and fire departments functioned much the same as their equivalents in other cities, the 911 dispatch center was also contracted out to a New Jersey-based company, ixP.

"Nothing about Sandy Springs hints that it is one of the country's purest examples of a contract city," noted the *Times'* David Segal. "Even those city hall employees betray no sign that they work for a jumble of corporations."[95]

For a number of years, it worked perfectly well that way. The city's balance sheet was positive and there was widespread consensus the novel approach to city services was working.

However, by 2019, city officials determined bringing many services in-house could actually be more cost-effective than contracting and decided to hire over 100 city employees. Additional hires followed.[96]

While this is a notable shift from the first 14 years of the city's approach, city officials emphasized they stood by their commitment to a combined approach of leveraging the private sector.

"[We] still use P3 [the public-private partnership] for a number of services, so we have adopted more of a hybrid P3/traditional model than a pure version of either delivery model, which has always been the case in Sandy Springs," Mayor Rusty Paul said in 2019. "We just shifted (we believe temporarily) more services to the traditional model due to the premium pricing that exists in the private sector today."[97]

For Austill Stuart of the Reason Foundation, the takeaway from Sandy Springs' experiment isn't that privatization doesn't work, but that having the flexibility to adjust to shifting circumstances is vital to properly serving the public.

"While Sandy Springs did more recently choose to insource most of its contracts, it's important to note they started out with a single contract where one company provided almost all government services, then the city found it could save more money by structuring competitive sourcing for smaller-scope service contracts," he points out. "So their model for contracting underwent evolution even before insourcing."[98]

Following this narrative of what happened in Sandy Springs, this isn't a knock on privatization or private-delivery of services per se, but an advantageous feature.

Further, according to Stuart, the city has retained some of its private-sector-influence. He continued, "The city...applies performance-based management practices to its employees, too, so they are somewhat managed how a private workforce in the same positions would be, even if they are public employees."[99]

Still, critics of reading too much into Sandy Springs' privatization experiment can rightly point out that, at the end of the day, the city returned to in-sourcing city functions because it apparently made financial sense to do so.

Additionally, there has been an ongoing criticism that Sandy Springs is unlike many cities. It's essentially a wealthier, whiter suburban city than most others in Georgia and in that sense there may indeed be limitations in how applicable Sandy Springs' model might be.

But, on the other hand, Sandy Springs did show that, in fact, it is possible for a sizable city to contract out a litany of city functions to private companies based from across the United States (from California to New Jersey) for a number of years.

The sky certainly didn't fall in Sandy Springs and unlike more traditionally structured cities which went bankrupt (like San Bernardino and Vallejo in California or Detroit, Mich.) didn't have to rush to change how it operated in a panic.

Start-up cities

The Lakewood Plan and Sandy Springs again aren't terribly far off from your standard city. But what if we thought about even more innovative approaches to municipal government?

Here, I return to the work of Chapman Law Professor Tom Bell, who has championed special jurisdictions as a framework for thinking differently about government, regulations and rulemaking. Such jurisdictions are all around us, big and small.[100]

At one level, there are common-interest developments, which include those governed by homeowners associations which privately establish and enforce rules and provide services.

At a higher level are special economic zones, which can be generally defined as "demarcated geographic areas contained within a country's national boundaries where the rules of business are different from those that prevail in the national territory."[101]

Among the most famous examples of SEZs is Hong Kong. Long exempt from the backwards and regressive rules of the communist Chinese state, Hong Kong was able to become a bastion for economic freedom. With less government, low taxes, and pro-market orientation, Hong Kong was able to become wealthy precisely because it didn't need to follow all of the rules that saddled the surrounding country.

But Bell has also worked in developing what it might look like if one took the framework of a special economic zone and within it allowed for private governance.

Over a decade ago, the Central American nation of Honduras authorized zonas de empleo y desarrollo económico (zones for employment and economic development) or ZEDEs, which authorized, with government approval, the formation of special zones in the country with considerable autonomy over administrative, judicial and regulatory matters. ZEDEs are also allowed to contract for services.[102]

Bell helped work on the legal development of Próspera, a private city in Honduras on the island of Roatán, which seeks to attract business and investment with an innovative approach to government.

Businesses who establish themselves in Próspera would be allowed to operate under an extraordinarily flexible regulatory code – they could either use the regulatory system of Honduras, any of the top countries of the Organisation for Economic Co-operation and Development, common law or they could draw up their own regulations and pitch them to Próspera. The private city also imposes low tax rates: a 5 percent income tax, 1 percent tax on business income, 2.5 percent sales tax and a 1 percent tax on land.[103]

Now, whether Próspera and the ZEDEs are able to succeed remains to be seen, though activity has already begun in Próspera. However, Honduras is an unstable Central American nation and recently the government there has sought to axe the ZEDEs.[104] Even so, Próspera argues it remains protected for the next 50 years by contract.[105]

The point here is not to suggest that we can replicate ZEDEs or even special economic zones like Hong Kong. Bell, for his part, has advocated for the creation of such zones on federally owned properties in the country.

But my point here is to raise some food for thought. What makes Hong Kong or the ZEDEs worth thinking about is that they reveal the shortcomings of their respective surrounding jurisdictions. Yet what they offer isn't all that complicated. Their advantages are freedom from political and regulatory constraints as well as lower taxes.

Some final thoughts

The fate of cities should not fall on city hall, but they often do.

Clear, easy-to-follow rules make it easier to get things done. Clunky rules laundered through bureaucracies and fiefdoms make it hard to get things done.

City officials and residents alike need to be honest with themselves. If you had the chance to write the rules and regulations of their city from scratch, would they look like the ones on the book today? Do the rules and regulations on the books today facilitate or hinder others from peacefully pursuing their own interests? Do city policies seem designed to favor or disfavor specific entities in a community?

If your answers are "No," "Hinder," and "Yes," you know your city needs to go back to the drawing board.

When it comes to services, a focus on service delivery for the best interests of city residents at the best price should be the default. But many cities seem to deliver services for the best interests of city employees.

When it comes to services some questions to consider: Are you getting your money's worth from your city's services? Could the private sector perform city operations at least as well at a lower cost?

I refer back to Bob Poole on the question of how to think about government-provided services.

"I think privatization is a tool that should always be available for governments to use," says Poole. "Reviewing the performance and cost of various public services should be done periodically, and where cost and performance look as if they might be improved, a competition in which the city workforce must put in its bid in competition with bids from outside providers (something former Indianapolis Mayor Steve Goldsmith pioneered) would be wise."[106]

The opportunity costs for being on the wrong side of well-written rules and competently delivered services are massive. They mean missing out on investment, jobs, additional funding for city needs, shutting out solutions to problems and delivering shoddier-quality services.

If we are going to live in freer, better cities, we need City Hall to know when to stay out of the way of free people trying to live their lives.

Endnotes

1   Andrew Meleta and Alex Montgomery, "Barriers to Business: How Cities Can Pave a Cheaper, Faster, and Simpler Path to Entrepreneurship," Institute for Justice, February 2022 https://ij.org/report/barriers-to-business/

2   Ibid.

3   Steven Greenhut, "Tax collectors bite taco trucks," *The Orange County Register*, July 14, 2012, https://www.ocregister.com/2012/07/14/steven-greenhut-tax-collectors-bite-taco-trucks/

4   Ruby de Luna, "Changes coming to Seattle food truck rules," KUOW, Aug. 25, 2022, https://www.sbsun.com/2020/09/15/new-85-bed-transitional-housing-complex-for-homeless-men-opens-in-san-bernardino/

5   City of Riverside website, https://riversideca.gov/press/riverside's-"one-stop-shop"-boosts-customer-service-welcomes-investment

6   City of Aurora, Colorado website, "Aurora: Here for Business," no date, https://www.auroragov.org/cms/one.aspx?pageId=18633183

7   Ibid.

8   Darcy Spears, "Officials in Nevada Demolish Tiny Homes Built for Homeless in Las Vegas," KTNV Las Vegas, Aug. 15, 2022, https://www.ktnv.com/13-investigates/officials-in-nevada-demolish-tiny-homes-built-for-homeless-in-las-vegas

9   Elizabeth Nolan Brown, "Tiny Homes for Las Vegas Homeless Demolished Over Code Violations," *Reason*, Aug. 23, 2022, https://reason.com/2022/08/23/tiny-homes-for-las-vegas-homeless-demolished-over-code-violations/

10   Brian Whitehead, "New 85-bed transitional housing complex for homeless men opens in San Bernardino," *San Bernardino Sun*, September 16, 2020, https://www.sbsun.com/2020/09/15/new-85-bed-transitional-housing-complex-for-homeless-men-opens-in-san-bernardino/

11   Mary's Mercy Center, Inc. website, http://www.marysmercy-center.org/MARYS-MERCY-CENTER-INC.html

12   Sal Rodriguez, "San Bernardino Council Might OK Homeless Shelter at Last ," *The Press-Enterprise*, Dec. 4, 2016, https://www.sbsun.com/2020/09/15/new-85-bed-transitional-housing-complex-for-homeless-men-opens-in-san-bernardino/

13   Ibid.

14   Ibid.

15   Alicia Robinson, "After years on good terms, homeless nonprofit sues Anaheim over permit denial," *Orange County Register*, Feb. 11, 2022, https://www.ocregister.com/2022/02/11/after-years-on-good-terms-homeless-nonprofit-sues-anaheim-over-permit-denial/

16   Sam Spiegelman and Jeremy Talcott, "Anaheim violates property rights to keep a women's shelter out of the city," *Orange County Register*, September 7, 2022, https://www.ocregister.com/2022/09/07/anaheim-violates-property-rights-to-keep-a-womens-shelter-out-of-the-city/

17   Tom Bell, *Your Next Government? From the Nation State to Stateless Nations*, Cambridge Univ. Press, 2018

18   Curt Pringle, "A Bias Towards Freedom: Freedom Breeds: Choice and Innovation in Anaheim," *Innovators In Action*, Reason Foundation, no date, https://www.scottsdaleaz.gov/AssetFactory.aspx?did=30720

19   City of Anaheim Regulatory Relief Task Force, "Phase 1 Recommendations" Report, Nov. 2011, https://www.anaheim.net/DocumentCenter/View/3773/Regulatory-Relief-Task-Force-?bidId=

20   Steven Greenhut, "Too Bad Anaheim Chose to Ignore its Better Angels, May 26, 2022, https://www.ocregister.com/2022/05/26/too-bad-anaheim-chose-to-ignore-its-better-angels/

21   Brandon Pho, "Santa Ana Moves Forward With Reduced Affordable Housing Requirements ," *Voice of OC*, Aug. 19, 2020, https://calmatters.org/commentary/2022/05/how-santa-ana-discourages-new-housing-with-hefty-fees/

22   Dan Walters, "How Santa Ana discourages new housing with hefty fees," *CalMatters*, May 11, 2022, https://calmatters.org/commentary/2022/05/how-santa-ana-discourages-new-housing-with-hefty-fees/

23   Ibid.

24   Ibid.

25   Robert Poole, *Cutting Back City Hall*, Universe Publishing, 1980

26   Ibid.
27   Lee Ohanian, "California State Government Workers Earn
      $143,000, Twice As Much As Private Sector Workers," *Hoover
      Institution*, Feb. 15 2022, https://www.hoover.org/research/califor-
      nia-state-government-workers-earn-143000-twice-much-private-
      sector-workers
28   No author, "Nevada local government workers the highest paid in
      the nation," Nov. 21 2018, https://www.thecentersquare.com/neva-
      da/nevada-local-government-workers-the-highest-paid-in-the-na-
      tion/article_8ed7cd54-e9e9-11e8-8448-3f1d0d869f41.html
29   Los Angeles 2020 Commission, "A Time for Truth," Dec. 2013,
      https://www.scribd.com/document/197373893/A-Time-for-Truth
30   Ibid.
31   Sarah Bohn, Caroline Danielson, and Patricia Malagon, "Poverty in
      California," Public Policy Institute of California, July 2021, https://
      www.ppic.org/publication/poverty-in-california/
32   Shannon Sedgwick, LA County and SoCal Forecast, presentation,
      Los Angeles County Economic Development Corporation, Feb.
      2020, https://laedc.org/wpcms/wp-content/uploads/2020/02/Shan-
      non-Sedgwick-SLIDES-LAEDC-2020-Forecast.pdf
33   Rick Cole, Gail Goldberg and Bud Ovrom, "Prevent Future L.A.
      City Council Scandals by Fixing Our Planning System," *Los
      Angeles Times*, Oct. 6 2020, https://www.latimes.com/opinion/sto-
      ry/2020-10-06/city-council-scandal-planning-reform
34   Ibid.
35   Joe Nation, "Pension Math: Public Pension Spending and Ser-
      vice Crowd Out in California, 2003-2030," Stanford Institute for
      Economic Policy Research, Oct. 2017, https://drive.google.com/
      file/d/1tBE6ILLGPJd0dtz8YugZlD1zvvcSdESP/view?usp=drives-
      dk
36   Ron Galperin, "The Problems and Progress of Prop. HHH," report,
      Los Angeles City Controller, Feb. 2022, https://lacontroller.org/
      audits-and-reports/problems-and-progress-of-prop-hhh/
37   Judge David O. Carter, preliminary injunction, LA Alliance for
      Human Rights, et al. v. City of Los Angeles, et al., April 20, 2021,
      https://s3.documentcloud.org/documents/20685175/judge-car-
      ter-april-20-2021-preliminary-injunction-la-alliance-for-human-
      rights-vs-city-of-la-et-all.pdf

38   Matt Welch, "L.A. to Sell Zoo, Convention Center?," *Reason Magazine*, March 19, 2009, https://reason.com/2009/03/19/la-to-sell-zoo-convention-cent/

39   Interview with author, August 2022

40   Ibid.

41   "Privatization of Some L.A. City Operations Urged," *Los Angeles Business Journal*, Dec. 21, 2008, https://labusinessjournal.com/news/privatization-of-some-la-city-operations-urged/

42   Ibid.

43   Interview with author, Aug. 2022

44   Press release, "The Los Angeles Convention Center Looks Back on Four Years with AEG Facilities," Los Angeles Convention Center, Dec. 6, 2017 https://www.lacclink.com/news/detail/the-los-angeles-convention-center-looks-back-on-four-years-with-aeg-facilities

45   Howard Fine, "Plan to Privatize L.A. Zoo Stopped," *Los Angeles Business Journal*, Sept. 27, 2012, https://labusinessjournal.com/tourism/plan-privatize-l-zoo-stopped/

46   Ron Galperin, "Greater Transparency and Accountability at L.A. Zoo," Audit report, Los Angeles City Controller, April 2018, https://lacontroller.org/audits-and-reports/greater-transparency-accountability-at-l-a-zoo/

47   Ibid.

48   Ibid.

49   Ibid.

50   Letter to L.A. Controller Ron Galperin, March 18, 2018, https://lacontroller.org/wp-content/uploads/2019/02/audit-2018-LA-Zoo.pdf

51   Robert Poole, *Cutting Back City Hall*, Universe Publishing, 1980

52   Ibid.

53   Email correspondence to author, August 2022

54   R3 Consulting Group, Inc., "Solid Waste and Recycling Program Review Economic and Strategic Study," report to the Riverside, California City Council, Dec. 23, 2019, https://riversideca.legistar.com/View.ashx?M=F&ID=7984429&GUID=0D-CFF15B-DBEB-4EBB-8A20-8D1B3DC4866B

55   Ryan Hagen, "San Bernardino bankruptcy: Trash collection outsourcing finalized," *San Bernardino Sun*, Jan. 26, 2016, https://www.sbsun.com/2016/01/26/san-bernardino-bankruptcy-trash-collection-outsourcing-finalized/

56   Ryan Hagen, "Riverside decides not to outsource trash collection," *The Press-Enterprise*, Jan. 16, 2020, https://www.pe.com/2020/01/16/riverside-decides-not-to-outsource-trash-collection/

57   Marc Joffe, "Local Governments in California Lost $20 Million in 2020 Running Public Golf Courses," *Orange County Register*, April 5, 2022, https://www.ocregister.com/2022/04/05/local-governments-in-california-lost-20-million-in-2020-running-public-golf-courses/

58   Adrian Moore, "A Sensible Path for Bobby Jones Golf Club," *yourobserver.com*, Sept. 22, 2016, https://www.yourobserver.com/article/sensible-path-bobby-jones-golf-club

59   Paul Gessing and D. Dowd Muska, "Fixing ABQ: Fiscal Policy," Policy Brief, Aug. 2017 https://riograndefoundation.org/downloads/rgf_abq_economic_reform.pdf

60   Marc Joffe, "Local Governments in California Lost $20 Million in 2020 Running Public Golf Courses," *Orange County Register*, April 5, 2022, https://www.ocregister.com/2022/04/05/local-governments-in-california-lost-20-million-in-2020-running-public-golf-courses/

61   "Airport Privatization: Issues and Options for Congress," Congressional Research Service, March 2021 https://sgp.fas.org/crs/misc/R43545.pdf

62   Peter Shawn Taylor, "It's Time to Privatize Canadian Airports," C2C Journal, Aug. 19, 2021, https://c2cjournal.ca/2021/08/its-time-to-privatize-canadian-airports/

63   "Airport Privatization: Issues and Options for Congress," Congressional Research Service, March 2021 https://sgp.fas.org/crs/misc/R43545.pdf

64   Joseph Guinto, "Privatizing Airports Is a No-Brainer," *The Atlantic*, Aug. 18, 2020, https://www.theatlantic.com/ideas/archive/2020/08/sell-airports/615331/

65   Robert Poole and Chris Edwards, "Privatizing U.S. Airports," Cato Institute, Nov. 21, 2016, https://www.cato.org/tax-budget-bulletin/ privatizing-us-airports

66   Rita Fahy, Ben Evarts and Gary P. Stein, "U.S. Fire Department Profile," National Fire Protection Association, Dec. 2021, https:// www.nfpa.org/-/media/Files/News-and-Research/Fire-statis- tics-and-reports/Emergency-responders/osfdprofile.pdf

67   Rita Fahy, Ben Evarts and Gary P. Stein, "U.S. Fire Department Profile, Supporting Tables," Table 20, National Fire Protection As- sociation, Dec. 2021, https://www.nfpa.org//-/media/Files/News- and-Research/Fire-statistics-and-reports/Emergency-responders/ osFDProfileTables.pdf

68   Nancy Poole, "Fire-Fighting for Profit," Foundation for Economic Education, Aug. 1, 1991, https://fee.org/articles/fire-fighting-for- profit/

69   Website of Rural Metro Fire, https://www.ruralmetrofire.com

70   Email correspondence, Sept. 2022

71   Ibid.

72   "Where's the Fire? Stop Sending Fire Trucks to Medical Calls," Orange County Grand Jury, May 20, 2022 https://www.ocgrandju- ry.org/pdfs/2021_2022_GJreport/2022-05-20_Where's_the_Fire_ Stop_Sending_Fire_Trucks_to_Medical_Calls.pdf

73   Ibid.

74   Ibid.

75   Spencer Custodio, "Placentia First OC City to Leave Fire Author- ity and Form its Own Fire Department," *Voice of OC*, June 5, 2019, https://voiceofoc.org/2019/06/placentia-first-oc-city-to-leave-fire- authority-and-form-its-own-fire-department/

76   Spencer Custodio, "Placentia Alleges OC Fire Authority Miscon- duct After City Leaves Agency," *Voice of OC*, June 28, 2019, https:// voiceofoc.org/2019/06/placentia-alleges-oc-fire-authority-miscon- duct-after-city-leaves-agency/

77   Ibid.

78   Steven Greenhut, "In state government, no good idea goes un- punished," *Orange County Register*, Oct. 15, 2020,   https://www. ocregister.com/2020/10/15/in-state-government-no-good-idea- goes-unpunished/

79   Luis Estevez, "Reimagining Fire and Paramedic Services in the 21st Century," *PM Magazine*, ICMA, July 1, 2022, https://icma.org/articles/pm-magazine/reimagining-fire-and-paramedic-services-21st-century

80   Duane Gang, "Supervisors oppose state bill that thwarts library privatization," *The Press-Enterprise*, April 6, 2011, https://www.pe.com/2011/04/06/riverside-county-supervisors-oppose-state-bill-that-thwarts-library-privatization/

81   Library Systems and Services, "The Story of Riverside County's Historic Partnership with LS&S, no date, https://www.lsslibraries.com/success-stories/riverside-county-library-system/

82   California Assembly Floor Analysis, Assembly Bill 438, Sept. 8, 2011

83   Duane Gang, "Supervisors oppose state bill that thwarts library privatization," *The Press-Enterprise*, April 6, 2011, https://www.pe.com/2011/04/06/riverside-county-supervisors-oppose-state-bill-that-thwarts-library-privatization/

84   California Assembly Floor Analysis, Assembly Bill 438, Sept. 8, 2011

85   Assembly Bill 438, State of California, Chaptered language, https://leginfo.legislature.ca.gov/faces/billNavClient.xhtml?bill_id=201120120AB438

86   Andrew Clark, "Council Unanimously Votes to Take Back Library Operations ," *The Signal*, Jan. 9, 2018, https://signalscv.com/2018/01/council-unanimously-votes-take-back-library-operations/

87   Email correspondence with author, Aug. 2022

88   Eric Westervelt, "Some California Cities Criminalize Nuisance Code Violations," *NPR*, Feb. 14, 2018, https://www.npr.org/2018/02/14/585122825/some-california-cities-criminalize-nuisance-code-violations

89   Ibid.

90   Institute for Justice, case update, https://ij.org/case/indio-fines/

91   Elaine Woo, "His Vision of Lakewood as a New Kind of City Created a Model Copied Nationwide," *Los Angeles Times*, Sept. 4, 2008, https://www.latimes.com/archives/la-xpm-2008-sep-04-me-todd4-story.html

92   City of Lakewood website, https://www.lakewoodcity.org/About/
      Our-History/The-Lakewood-Plan

93   Geoffrey Segal, "The Real Sandy Springs Effect," *Reason Founda-
      tion*, Dec. 2, 2005, https://reason.org/commentary/the-real-sandy-
      springs-effect/

94   David Segal, "A Georgia Town Takes the People's Business
      Private ," *New York Times*, June 23, 2012, https://www.nytimes.
      com/2012/06/24/business/a-georgia-town-takes-the-peoples-busi-
      ness-private.html

95   Ibid.

96   John Ruch, "Is Sandy Springs' Privatization Shift a Big Risk or No
      Big Deal?," *Reporter Newspapers & Atlanta Intown*, June 22, 2019,
      https://reporternewspapers.net/2019/06/22/is-sandy-springs-pri-
      vatization-shift-a-big-risk-or-no-big-deal/

97   Ibid.

98   Email correspondence, Aug. 2022

99   Ibid.

100   Interview with author, Aug. 2022

101   Tom Bell, *Your Next Government? From the Nation State to Stateless
      Nations*, Cambridge Univ. Press, 2018

102   Ryan Berg and Henry Ziemer, "What Are the Zones for Em-
      ployment and Economic Development in Honduras?," Center for
      Strategic & International Studies, April 27, 2022, https://reason.
      com/2022/04/27/honduras-ends-its-experiment-with-charter-cit-
      ies/

103   Próspera website, https://prospera.hn

104   Brian Doherty, "Honduras Ends Its Experiment With Charter
      Cities," *Reason*, April 27, 2022, https://reason.com/2022/04/27/
      honduras-ends-its-experiment-with-charter-cities/

105   Bell interview with author, August 2022

106   Email correspondence, August 2022

About the Author

Sal Rodriguez

Sal Rodriguez is a PRI senior fellow and the opinion editor for the Southern California News Group, a group of 11 newspapers in Los Angeles County, Orange County, Riverside County and San Bernardino County. He first joined the newspaper business in 2014 as an editorial writer and columnist for the *Orange County Register* and the *Riverside Press-Enterprise*.

Prior to joining the newspaper business, he worked with Solitary Watch, investigating the use and abuse of solitary confinement, and wrote about issues ranging from criminal justice reform to pension reform for the Reason Foundation.

About Pacific Research Institute

The Pacific Research Institute (PRI) champions freedom, opportunity, and personal responsibility by advancing free-market policy solutions. It provides practical solutions for the policy issues that impact the daily lives of all Americans, and demonstrates why the free market is more effective than the government at providing the important results we all seek: good schools, quality health care, a clean environment, and a robust economy.

Founded in 1979 and based in San Francisco, PRI is a non-profit, non-partisan organization supported by private contributions. Its activities include publications, public events, media commentary, community leadership, legislative testimony, and academic outreach.

Center for Business and Economics

PRI shows how the entrepreneurial spirit—the engine of economic growth and opportunity—is stifled by onerous taxes, regulations, and lawsuits. It advances policy reforms that promote a robust economy, consumer choice, and innovation.

Center for Education

PRI works to restore to all parents the basic right to choose the best educational opportunities for their children. Through research and grassroots outreach, PRI promotes parental choice in education, high academic standards, teacher quality, charter schools, and school-finance reform.

Center for the Environment

PRI reveals the dramatic and long-term trend toward a cleaner, healthier environment. It also examines and promotes the essential ingredients for abundant resources and environmental quality: property rights, markets, local action, and private initiative.

Center for Health Care

PRI demonstrates why a single-payer Canadian model would be detrimental to the health care of all Americans. It proposes market-based reforms that would improve affordability, access, quality, and consumer choice.

Center for California Reform

The Center for California Reform seeks to reinvigorate California's entrepreneurial self-reliant traditions. It champions solutions in education, business, and the environment that work to advance prosperity and opportunity for all the state's residents.

Center for Medical Economics and Innovation

The Center for Medical Economics and Innovation aims to educate policymakers, regulators, health care professionals, the media, and the public on the critical role that new technologies play in improving health and accelerating economic growth.

Free Cities Center

The Free Cities Center cultivates innovative ideas to improve our cities and urban life based around freedom and property rights – not government.

www.ingramcontent.com/pod-product-compliance
Lightning Source LLC
Chambersburg PA
CBHW070030030426
42335CB00017B/2365